Devils
In
America

This book is written not to be
controversial
But
To enlighten the minds of those who have
the ability
To broaden their minds in a
Different Direction.

Devils
In
America

ISBN 978-0-9858029-1-2

Devils in America

Author's Background

I was born in a small North Florida town named Jennings. I dated and married my high school sweetheart Reatha Mitchell. We have four beautiful daughters, educated and doing well.

Reatha and I had good paying jobs over the years.
With these good paying jobs we forgot where we came from and let the Devil come into our life.

With the Devil in our lives it destroyed our marriage. Today we both agree that is one of the worst things that can happen in a marriage. The worst thing is not having God in your life.

Dedication

To my Loving Mother
Rosia Mae Gandy

&

My Children
Deborah D. Gates
Donna D. Wilkerson
Dayatra D. Arnold
D'Shawn D. Watts

&

Nephew
Jimmy Hawkins

Contents

Chapter I

World made for us

God made the world for us. We did not make it for him. Therefore everything we do should be in the name of the Lord

Parents, Supervisors, Doctors or Judges should do things in the name of God and not man. When we do things for our family or friends we should make sure it the right thing for us to do.

God respect us to reflect his nature. All our teaching should reflect God's nature. All our workmanship should reflect God's nature.

Everything we do should be in the name of the Lord. This is God's world and we should abide by his teaching.

Chapter II

Works of Satan

Satan is very smart. He does things in ways you
wouldn't recognize until it too late. He place
people in key positions to do what he desires.
When it does happen we are too ashamed to go
back and correct it.

The separation of church and state was the Devil's best
accomplishment. He removed the spiritually minds from making
laws and standing up for the righteously. He promise them
richness and success.

Then he went on and took the prayers out our schools. This set
the stage for the Devils to rein and take our children with him.
He had his rules makers to make laws where you cannot
discipline your own child.

Listen to the news; every station mention disasters. The children
we taught to pray can't because the law says no. Instead they
have taken up weapons killing each other. There is no discipline
for them to honor. The devil has them and we let this happen.

Chapter III

American Revolution

This country is divided. It is an ugly revolution
between Republicans and Democrats.

.

I am sad because I love this country. I want the
best for this country. But the last Presidential
election and voices afterward made me very sad.

The fight between Republicans and Democrats
are very frightening. Just in the last election; a
new elected person stated "His voyage is getting
rid of the President". I could not believe I heard
that. If anyone felt that way he should be
ashamed to say it.

The people voted him in and no one question his
statement. I watch television and I hear Ministers
giving ugly statements about our President. Yes,
I believe Satan have taken over.

How in the world do you expect a country to be successful with
these types of attitudes?

.

God have been good to this Country. The goodness of forgiveness and holiness is gone. There is nothing left but a very few that understand what to expect from this type of governing body. They are not surprise because they are saved and know what happens to governments when the people elect devils to guide them. **READ YOUR BIBLE!!!**

I truly wish that this country could regain her strength again. It would almost impossible to get rid of the Devils the people have elected. They are wealthy and confident you will believe what they say. They want to be your Master.

This book is written to open America's mind as to what have happen in the past years. Also, what is going to happen to us if we continue down this ugly past?

Chapter IV

New Leaders Needed

We need God fearing leaders and Judges to lead this country.

What am I speaking about?

Look at America's situations. We have so many controversial decisions. These decisions should tell us their Makers are not qualified in their positions.

Let us start from the beginning: The church made the state; not the state made the church.

What does that suppose to tell you? This should tell you that the voice of the state should come from the church.

Can I prove this? Yes I can.

The Lord gave Jehoshaphat great power. He ruled over the land of Edom, over Philistines and the entire wilderness in the south. Jehoshaphat chose judges that sit on the right side of the Lord. He told them (Judges) "I want you all to remember; you are not judging for man, but for the Lord".

There you see all our Judges should be judging for the Lord and not man.

The Bible tells us in the latter days Men shall depart from the faith, giving heed to seducing spirits and doctrines of devils. This means the rich falls into temptation and a snare and become engage in many foolish and hurtful lusts.

We should be vigilante not to let the rich lead us away from God's way.

I heard a man on television speaking about how we should keep our Army strong. He speaks like a devil. Your strength comes from the Lord and not the Army. He should have said how to keep America spiritual strong;

Read your bible: Strength comes from the Lord. The size of the Army does not constitute righteousness. If you are right you will win the war.

Think America is the great city that reign over the earth. This city also is the habitation of devils. Therefore when God looks down here he sees all this ugliness and guess what is going to happen?

He is going to send the lamb to destroy you. This big Army will not defend you against the word of God. The Army will lose and we will be destroyed.

What we have is the Devil has divided this country. The fight between the Republications and Democrats are ungodly. We laugh with the devil when this is going on and he sending us to hell.

What America need is togetherness. Separation is useless and you will fall in a long run. We need something to keep us together and as we the people can control. Today things are out of control and believe me it will be a tough fight to get things together.

First thing we need to do is get rid of Republican and Democrat party. We should have one party probably named The American Party. The American Party will be the voice of the people and not someone telling the people what to do.

The American Party which will be the people set rules for everyone to follow. A person who is rich cannot see the needs of a poor person. Therefore a rich person is useless in a top seat. Keep them out and place moderate income godly people to look after your interest.

If you were an accused would you rather go before Satan or a godly person for sentencing?

Chapter V

An untold story
Part I

This is a two part story I want to tell you.

Long ago there was this Judge. Before him came a middle age woman who was charged with embezzlement.

As the Prosecutor presented his case the Judge notice tears running down this woman cheeks.

When both attorneys finish their opening statements; he calls both parties in his office.

Once inside his office he asked this woman "Tell me what happened."

The woman began to speak. "I used to own my grandmother house. Six years ago my husband persuaded me to buy a new house. Four months ago he left me and the children for another woman. He has not helped us and we are waiting on the Courts to make him take care of his children. I have a record

of the amount of money I taken to help us survive. It took $100.00 each week and I planned to repay when the court help us. Now I do not have a job and me and the children will be evicted"
More tears rolls down her cheeks.

The Judge sits silently a few minutes, looking at both attorneys and the accused.

Then he spoke: "I tell you what I am going to do; (speaking to the accused) I am going to pay your company the money you took, I am going to speak with your manager to see if he will give you your job back, now (speaking to the attorneys) when we get back in the courtroom I will dismiss this case."

The Prosecutor jumps sky high. "Your Honor!! You cannot do this; this woman is accused of embezzlement. If this happen every embezzler will try to get off."

The Judge looked at him and reply: "look on my wall. You do not see all the plaques of colleges and Universities I attended. You only see one and will you please read it for me."

10

The Prosecutor walks over to the plaque and reads; "Honorary degree from My Lord and savior Jesus Christ"

The Prosecutor turned around slowly and took a strange look at the Judge. Without saying a word he rushed back outside.

The look on the Prosecutor's face told it all. The Devil met Christ at the crossings.

The Judge went back into the courtroom and dismissed the case.

How many Judges, Parents, teachers, bosses, etc; have this degree hanging in their office?

Please believe me; with this hanging on your wall, mind and in your heart you cannot fail. God will always be with you. Keep this crown of righteousness and you will be the happiest person in the world.

This crown of righteousness should be upon every parent, every Judge, every President and everyone with authority over another. If it's not there, there is trouble forthcoming.

I will tell you the rest of this embezzlement story at the end of this book. (cont'd)

11

Chapter VI

Devil's Work Sums Up

The Devil is very, very smart. He is slowly eradicating all the things that remind us we have a Savior in Heaven.

He divided the church and state. Common sense should tell us we need ones with Godly experience to guide a country. Who wants the Devil to guide them? You cannot have it both ways: You are godly or ungodly. There isn't anything between. Read your Bible all the great kings were connected to God.

The Devil took the prayer out of schools. He started on the people at an early age. Look around you; all the school shooting and dope in schools. We did not have this when prayer was allowed.

All these kids walking the streets, stealing and selling dope is the results. There is no discipline near them.

We had a good way to teach our children and guess what? The devil made rules where you cannot discipline your own child.

Why? He wanted them; he knows if this child isn't taught a decent living, she or he belongs to him. And that is true; all you have to do is look around you. There is never a "yes sir or no sir". No respect is in sight.

Why is all this happening? We as Christians sit back on our lazy behinds and complain to no one. We get among our friends and make like we are brilliant and know everything.

The devil has his people in place and they are choosing ungodly ideas to satisfy Satan. We have not considered the possibility of losing our way of living.

There is no difference between one dictator leading your country or a group of Satan dictators leading. They all have the same agenda.

They make you think they are out to help you to get your vote. Be wise and ask yourself why this man wants to lead this country?

Let me tell you this; if I was a rich man why would I waste my time acting Presidential unless I had a special agenda. Think America!!! Do not wait any longer; we must make good choices for our future.

Let me tell you again. On the last election I heard one Senator say; "My only job is to get rid of the President." Why in the world would you want this devil in the White House? He told you who he is and no one complained because he supposed to be one at the top.

We are his boss and we should not allow this to go on. If we do we are guilty as well. When the country heard this we should have demanded he resign. We have removed people before; why not this one? Because he is saying something Satan wants you to believe is the right thing to do.

People of America please listen. We need middle income godly people to lead us. If they do not believe in God they are known to make bad decisions.

14

Making bad decisions cause problems that many suffers. They do not care if people suffer. If they cared Satan would not let them be there.

Once again I am asking Americans to sit back and think. That is your right to think what is best for your country. Do not think and want certain decisions to hurt your neighbors or a different nationality. You will lose in the end. The Bible said it and you better believe it.

What we have now is the rich making all the noise on how he is going to help you. He is going to help keep you poor. The rich cannot understand my needs. You have to be poor to understand this.

Let me tell you something else. Remember US Steel? Do you remember Bethlehem Steel? Those so call leaders of ours took our jobs and sent them overseas.

Money is the reason why! I said this all along; most people in power love to make their pockets fat. They make decisions to make their pockets fat and we get our empty. Every American company should be made to make things in America.

15

Let me tell what I know. I drove trucks for a long time. I pick up loads of steel and take it different places.

This time I picked up a load of steel from the docks. I notice the water marks on it but that has nothing to do with my delivery. I was assigned to take it to a sheet metal company.

When I took the metal there the boss look at it and was surprised at it condition. He had his men to unload the truck. The metal was unloaded and I left.

A few months later I went back with a load of US Steel.
The boss came out and said; "You remember that load of steel you delivered here?" I said "Yes Sir" He went on: "That metal was for a building at the Naval Air Station" He paused."We prepared all that metal for duck work and had put most of up in the building at NAS".

He paused; "Then an Inspector came around and made us tear it all out".

I said "What!" He continued "That job call for domestic metal and that was foreign metal"

16

"What now" I said. He said "That salesman tried to make his pockets fat, now his company is going to lose money."

There you see some smart idiot fresh out of college though he knew his job and cost his company a lot of money.

I have reason to believe when he was hired his resume looked good to his boss. His boss thought this guy would make his company a lot of money.

Every country needs steel factories. We had two that should be doing great. Some smart devil wanted to fatten his pocket and made the decision our factories should close down.

Many people lost homes and almost everything because the steel factories closed down. Who is going to stop them?

That is the reason why we need godly people leading us. The Government should have stepped in and took over. If this would have happen all the steel factories would still be running.

The devil got you thinking this is a private enterprise, not government business and butt out. This is the reason we need godly people running this country. They would have recognized many people would suffer if these mills close.

Many families thru generation have worked at these mills. Their father, grandfather and great grandfather worked there and they planned to work there also.

The devil makes us make many mistakes running after money. Most times when there is an issue; money is involved.

Many of our people are out of work because companies want to make excess money. They should know God will bless them if they do the right thing.

Let me tell you about my county. We have a great city counsel and wonderful school board members.

When the decision came where this county needed a school superintendent they went out of state to get one.

18

I could not believe our board members think the educators here in this big city does not have the qualifications to be over our children.

They went and got some guy from another state and put him over our school system. They also paid him an excellent contract.

Within six months after this guy got on the job everyone was dissatisfied with his decisions.

He had our children standing on the streets early in the mornings when it was dark. He had some walking as far as ten blocks to get to a bus stop. He was destroying our good system that was working.

This county finally had to let him go but he still was getting paid. That was a bad decision for our members made.

Can you see why all this was happening? There was no one that had the faith of our Lord. They made bad decisions because they did not ask him for answers.

Many people here suffered because our Lord was not included in their decisions.

It is very important to have someone with the wisdom of God to lead you. Not because I have made a million dollars and cheated most people to get it.

Believe me if someone make a lot of money someone is getting cheated. It not smart because in the long run you will lose. It might be cancer, painful illness or a love one deceased. You will lose in the end.

Therefore I beg Americans to not look at the race of a person. Look at his standing with the Holy Bible. If he is not in it we all will lose.

Not many people will speak like this; either they are afraid or do not understand the power of our Father.

They may also want to serve man and his ungodly wishes. Either way it will be a disaster for him and all around his family.

We have many nationalities here in the state. Why cannot we show the world what the United States is about? If we love each other like God intended for mankind our problems would be solved.

The hate groups will have to hate somewhere else. We should not let them chose the way for us to live. Think America! If you want a great country support this idea and bring love to all Americans.

If Americans do this I am sure God will cool the summers, warm the winters, stop the floods, hold the hurricanes and take care of our children.

Other countries will see the value of God in our lives and model after us. You see, we not only bless ourselves but bless other countries as well.

Chapter VII

What we must do

Let us look at another important issue. Our Supreme Court; The Supreme Court should be a group of Holy People. It is scary to see an unholy person on the Supreme Court. An unholy person might do anything. You would have hope for a good answer from a holy source. Look at the some decisions which have been down. Ungodly and awful and we are the cause.

Let us talk about money. You already know money is the roots of evil. All those in Congress that are taking money to vote one way or the other are of the Devil.

We the people should make sure this is not the way to go. Get all those that accepts money out. They are of the Devil and doing us no good but making their pockets fat. We are their boss; fire them!!!!

I want to congratulate President Clinton for balancing our budget.

I cannot congratulate the Republican afterward because they went behind him, made a mess and got us in all this debt.

The hard part people want to blame the Democrats who had nothing to do with this debt. Blame the President who made the debt.

I sit and listen to reporters and announcers who always say, "This President isn't doing anything". Do you think all of us are crazy? You look stupid saying that because you should know how this debt got there.

Everyone can see Devils carrying this speech. Believe me you really look like the devil when you say such and should know better.

I happen to be listening to the 700 Club one day and behold!! Pat Roberson said the ugliest thing I ever heard. He downed the Democrats and talked ugly about Obama.

I sent him an email and told him how ugly that was. He is supposed to be teaching love and how to keep America spiritually. He here downing the President and the President just got there. I do not watch the 700 Club anymore.

Now I understand why he wants to be President. Power!! Listen folks if God call someone to preach; that is the highest post in world. Although you would not understand this if you were not called.

Read your bible; if God select one to do a command; that is the highest you can get. He not only calls you but give you a weapon and protection from Satan.

We have so many Preachers that are out there for the money. God didn't call them. They called themselves for a job they are not entitled to.

Look around you. These Ministers are committing all kind of sin. You are at this church and the Pastor looking at this cute young girl or finding ways to fatten his pockets. This is shameful and disgraceful.

I went to my friend church one Sunday. When I walked in things just wasn't right.

The first seat I reached a lady was sitting in the middle. Her dress was so short I could almost see her underwear. The lady next to her had on skin tight pants. I said to myself this must be a night club.

This type of thing I see in many churches. There is no respect for Holy grounds. How is God going to bless this church with this type of things taking place? Deacons and Deaconesses should make sure God's house keep respectful things in place.

One friend I know told me he has to preach what the people want to hear. He speaks like they change Pastors quickly if he does something different.

I had to shake my head because I believe if God call a man to preach he also gives them a weapon. They should not fear what Satan done. He should do what God tell him and he will be rewarded.

Americans please listen; God is the only way for this country to get delivered. All those that want you to believe they know how to get us out of this mess. (Especially the rich) "I been in business and made million and I can make millions for you" Don't be a fool and fall for that gimmit.

They are lying. Just think a little bit for yourself. Think about what is going on. The rich is getting richer and the poor getting poorer.

The devil got you thinking its fun to see the Democrats and Republicans fight. We can stop this and if we do not do anything and thinking somehow it is not going to affect you; you are wrong.

(Untold story cont'd)

Let me finish the embezzlement case. The Judge did pay out his pocket the money the company was missing. He also told his story to the owner of the company.

The owner was shocked at what the Judge had done. His reply; "I will not only give her job back, I will boost her pay up $100.00 to help her make it" They both hugged in the name of God.

Immediately this company starts growing. Orders were coming from everywhere. In one year this company had grown seven time it size. God blessed this company

This happen many years ago and this company grew to one of the largest in the states. The name was changed and was sold for millions.

The Judge who started it all; he lived a full healthy life still helping and giving advice for ninety some years.

Now Americans do not be afraid to stand up for God. He will bless you, your children and grand children.

We all know what God laws are. Let's demand they be put into play. Do not let the ungodly destroy us.

One question I want to leave with you:
Are our Ministers, Pastors and TV people afraid to speak out? Are they afraid of their jobs or do they believe?

I

Special Poetry

In this book I will include two of my first
poems written in 1984.and 1991

Copyrighted 1984: by American Poetry
Association.
ISBN 0-88147-008-2
International Standard Serial Number:
0734-5135

Side of the Road

Here I stand on the side of the road
Scorned thru days and nights of cold
Brutalized by conditions often in despair
Criticized by the fortunate, to roads lead
elsewhere.

My future is uncertain, all bills are unpaid
Distress by the brain; overworked, tense,
hair fully grayed.
Depressed by the strain, evidence of the
heavy loads

Please don't leave me hear on the side of
the road.

Oh! Disappearing friends and prosperous
diplomats!
With perforated minds, fame and truth to
combat
Celebrating unclean fortunes; proudly as
you strode
Neglecting the innocence on the side of
the road

My legs are weak and a great feel of thirth
My eyes for sleep; understanding at its
worst
Misfit, unfit, scum, no good; all I've called
Located here on the side of the road.

Oh God! Suspend my death; preserve my
faith
Purify my breath, your word I'll never
forsake
I'm still, fulfill, thrill; your grace I behold
Patiently waiting here on the side of the
road:

Copyrighted 1991
ISBN Number 0-910147-18-3
Library of Congress Number 90-071398

Old Raggedy House

Thanks for this old raggedy house
Quiet, peaceful, even without a mouse
Weather changes bring a little pain
That cold wind and summer rain

Rags and paper plugged in the holes
Does a good job keeping out the cold
Ooh! Here comes a hard rain!
Pots and pans! Again and again
Catching all the water I can.

31

www.ingramcontent.com/pod-product-compliance
Lightning Source LLC
Chambersburg PA
CBHW030314030426
42337CB00012B/700